# Psalms Alive

## by Wendy English

Copyright © 2022 Wendy English. All rights reserved.
ISBN: 979-8-9864106-1-6
Fonts and graphics licensed through Canva and Adobe

*Dedicated to my dear mother, Donna, and treasured friend, Vicki.
May you both know the beauty of the gardens of your
lives that blossom with humility, faith & grace.*

# Creation Speaks

God's creation whispers his name and proclaims his unfailing love everywhere you look! Every bird, every flower, each sunrise, and sunset reflect the essence and beauty of our amazing God. Each day awakens his fresh mercy and exhales his faithfulness as the sun goes down. Where morning dawns and evening fades God calls forth songs of joy, and he sings them over us! Even the sparrow builds her nest to be close to God.

I love him because he lifts me out of the pit and calls me by name. He takes great delight in you and me and longs to quiet our anxious hearts with his love. He longs to be close to us.

May you feel his peaceful presence as you read these Psalms with the flowers and creatures he has made. And as you lay your head to rest when the day is done, may you hear him call your name too and remind you he is near.

"The Lord is compassionate and gracious, slow to anger and abounding in love."

Psalms 103:8

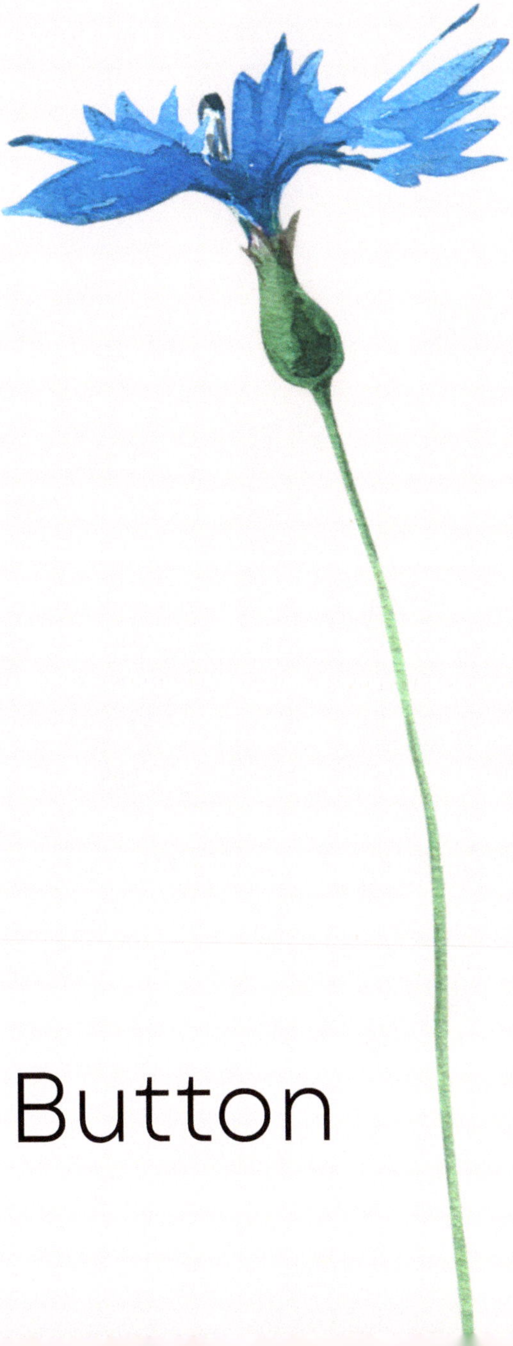

Bachelor Button

"Blessed is the one... whose delight
is in the law of the Lord,
and who meditates on
his law day and night.
That person is like a tree
planted by streams of water,
which yields its fruit in season
and whose leaf does not wither—
whatever they do prospers."

Psalms 1:2-3

Lavender

"But you, Lord,
are a shield around me,
my glory, the One
who lifts my head high.
I call out to the Lord,
and he answers me
from his holy mountain.
I lie down and sleep;
I wake again, because
the Lord sustains me."

Psalms 3:3-5

Dianthus

# Forget-Me-Not

"But I trust in your unfailing love;
my heart rejoices in your salvation.
I will sing the Lord's praise,
for he has been good to me."

Psalms 13:5-6

"The heavens declare
the glory of God;
the skies proclaim the
work of his hands.
Day after day
they pour forth speech;
night after night
they reveal knowledge."

Psalms 19:1-2

*Chamelaucium*

"May the words of my mouth and
the meditation of my heart
be pleasing in your sight,
Lord, my Rock and my Redeemer."

Psalms 19:14

Pensemon

"The Lord is my shepherd, I lack nothing.
He makes me lie down in green pastures.
He leads me beside quiet waters.
He refreshes my soul.
He guides me along the right paths
for his name's sake."

Psalms 23:1-3

*Lilly of the Valley*

"You are my hiding place; you will protect me from trouble and surround me with songs of deliverance."

Psalms 32:7

*Daisies*

"The Lord is close to the brokenhearted
and saves those who are crushed in spirit.
The righteous person may have many troubles,
but the Lord delivers him from them all."

Psalms 34:18-19

Blue Flax

"Take delight in the Lord,
and he will give you
the desires of your heart."

Psalms 37:4

Dalia

"I waited patiently
for the Lord;
he turned to me
and heard my cry.
He lifted me
out of the slimy pit,
out of the mud and mire;
he set my feet
on a rock and
gave me a firm
place to stand."

Psalms 40:1-2

*Calendula*

"As the deer pants for streams of water,
so my soul pants for you, my God.
My soul thirsts for God, for the living God."

Psalms 42:1-2

*Tulips*

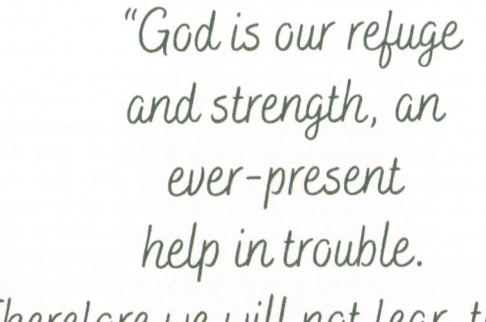

"God is our refuge
and strength, an
ever-present
help in trouble.
Therefore we will not fear, though
the earth give way
and the mountains fall
into the heart of the sea."

Psalms 46: 1-2

Oriental Poppy

"Be still, and know that I am God."

Psalms 46:10

Sunflower

# Meadow Sage

"Evening, morning and noon
I cry out in distress,
and he hears my voice.
He rescues me unharmed
from the battle waged against me,
even though many oppose me."

Psalms 55:17-18

"Cast your cares on the Lord
and he will sustain you;
he will never let the righteous be shaken."

Psalms 55:22

Lilac

"When I am afraid,
I put my trust in You."

Psalms 56:3

Clover

"Because your love is better than life,
my lips will glorify you.
I will praise you as long as I live,
and in your name I will lift up my hands."

Psalms 63:3-4

Cosmos

"The whole earth is filled with awe at your wonders;
where morning dawns, where evening fades,
you call forth songs of joy."

Psalms 65:8

# Raspberry Blossom

"A father to the fatherless, a defender of widows, is God in his holy dwelling. God sets the lonely in families, he leads out the prisoners with singing."

Psalms 68:5-6

Yellow Rose

"I will sing of the Lord's great love forever;
with my mouth I will make your faithfulness
known through all generations.
I will declare that your love stands firm forever,
that you have established
your faithfulness in heaven itself."

Psalms 89:1-2

*Daffodils*

"Teach us to number our days,
that we may gain a heart of wisdom."

Psalms 90:12

Geranium

# Garden Phlox

*"Whoever dwells in the shelter of the Most High will rest in the shadow of the Almighty."*

Psalms 91:1

"Shout for joy to the Lord, all the earth. Worship the Lord with gladness; come before him with joyful songs."

Psalms 100:1-2

Blue Hydrangea

"Praise the Lord, my soul,
and forget not
all his benefits—
who forgives all your sins
and heals all your diseases,
who redeems your
life from the pit
and crowns you with
love and compassion,
who satisfies your desires
with good things
so that your youth is
renewed like the eagle's."

Psalms 103:2-5

*Cornflower*

"Even the sparrow has found a home,
and the swallow a nest for herself,
where she may have her young—
a place near your altar, Lord Almighty,
my King and my God."

Psalms 84:3

Baby's Breath

"I love the Lord; for he heard my voice
he heard my cry for mercy.
Because he turned his ear to me,
I will call on him as long as I live!"

Psalms 116:1-2

## Pansies

"This is the day the Lord has made.
Let us rejoice and be glad in it."

Psalms 118:24

Hyacinth

# Freesia

"I wait for the Lord,
my whole being waits,
and in his word
I put my hope.
I wait for the Lord
more than watchmen
wait for the morning,
more than watchmen
wait for the morning.
Israel, put your hope
in the Lord,
for with the Lord is
unfailing love
and with him is
full redemption."

Psalms 130:5-7

# Poppy

"Give thanks to the Lord, for he is good. His love endures forever."

Psalms 136:1

"You have searched me, Lord,
and you know me.
You know when I sit and when I rise;
you perceive my thoughts from afar.
You discern my going out and my lying down;
you are familiar with all my ways." Psalms 139:1

## Queen Anne's Lace

"Search me, God, and know my heart;
test me and know my anxious thoughts.
See if there is any offensive way in me,
and lead me in the way everlasting."

Psalms 139:23-24

*Peony*

"Let each generation tell its children
of your mighty acts;
let them proclaim your power.
I will meditate on your majestic,
glorious splendor
and your wonderful miracles."

Psalms 145:4-5

*Wild Rose*

"He heals the brokenhearted
and binds up their wounds.
He determines the number of the stars
and calls them each by name."

Psalms 147:3-4

Pink Aster

"Let everything that has breath praise the Lord. Praise the Lord."

Psalms 150:6